Everyday Sparks

Barkon Legesse

Published by Barkon Legesse, 2024.

While every precaution has been taken in the preparation of this book, the publisher assumes no responsibility for errors or omissions, or for damages resulting from the use of the information contained herein.

EVERYDAY SPARKS

First edition. October 29, 2024.

Written by Barkon Legesse.

Table of Content

Introduction.______4

Chapter 1: The Nature of Inspiration.________10

◇ Defining inspiration and its role in human creativity
◇ The psychology behind inspirational moments
◇ How inspiration impacts personal growth and innovation

Chapter 2: Awakening to the Ordinary.______15

◇ Recognizing the extraordinary in everyday experiences
◇ Techniques for developing a more observant mindset
◇ Case studies of individuals who found inspiration in mundane situations

Chapter 3: Nature's Muse.______20

◇ Exploring the natural world as a source of inspiration
◇ Techniques for connecting with nature in urban environments
◇ How nature-inspired innovations have shaped human progress

Chapter 4: The Art of Seeing.______25

◇ Developing a keen eye for visual inspiration
◇ Techniques for finding inspiration in art, architecture, and design
◇ Exercises to enhance visual perception and creativity

Chapter 5: The Power of Human Connections.______30

◇ How relationships and interactions can spark inspiration
◇ Techniques for meaningful conversations and active listening
◇ Stories of collaborations that led to groundbreaking ideas

Chapter 6: The Soundscape of Inspiration.________37

◇ Finding inspiration in music, sounds, and silence
◇ Techniques for active listening and sound awareness
◇ How auditory experiences can enhance creativity and problem-solving

Chapter 7: Literary Landscapes.________42

◈ Drawing inspiration from books, poetry, and storytelling
◈ Techniques for creative reading and writing
◈ How literature can broaden perspectives and spark new ideas

Chapter 8: Digital Realms of Inspiration.______47

◈ Navigating online platforms for inspirational content
◈ Balancing digital inspiration with real-world experiences
◈ Techniques for curating a personalized digital inspiration board

Chapter 9: Overcoming Creative Blocks.________51

◈ Identifying common barriers to inspiration
◈ Strategies for breaking through mental obstacles
◈ Developing resilience and maintaining motivation

Chapter 10: Cultivating an Inspired Life.________56

◈ Integrating inspiration-seeking practices into daily routines
◈ Creating personal rituals for sustained creativity
◈ Techniques for sharing and spreading inspiration to others

Conclusion.

EveryDay Speaks

Introduction

Have you ever stopped to consider the extraordinary potential hidden within the ordinary moments of your day? As you sip your morning coffee, commute to work, or take an evening stroll, countless sparks of inspiration surround you, waiting to ignite your creativity and transform your perspective. In "Everyday Sparks: Finding Inspiration in the Commonplace," we embark on a journey to uncover the wellspring of inspiration that exists in the world around us, often overlooked in the hustle and bustle of daily life.

Inspiration is the lifeblood of human creativity and innovation. It fuels our passions, drives our ambitions, and propels us toward new horizons of possibility. Yet, in our fast-paced, technology-driven world, we often find ourselves searching for inspiration in grand gestures and extraordinary experiences, neglecting the wealth of inspiration that lies in the seemingly mundane aspects of our everyday lives. This book challenges that notion, inviting readers to rediscover the magic in the ordinary and tap into the boundless creative potential that surrounds us at every moment.

Drawing from a diverse range of disciplines including psychology, neuroscience, art, literature, and nature studies, "Everyday Sparks" offers a fresh perspective on the nature of inspiration and its profound impact on personal growth and societal progress. By exploring the intricate relationship between our environment, our senses, and our creative faculties, this book unveils the hidden connections that can spark revolutionary ideas and transformative insights.

What sets "Everyday Sparks" apart is its practical approach to cultivating inspiration in daily life. Rather than presenting inspiration as an elusive, lightning-bolt moment reserved for the gifted few, this book demystifies the process of finding and

Have you ever stopped to consider the extraordinary potential hidden within the ordinary moments of your day? As you sip your morning coffee, commute to work, or take an evening stroll, countless sparks of inspiration surround you, waiting to ignite your creativity and transform your perspective. In "Everyday Sparks: Finding Inspiration in the Commonplace," we embark on a journey to uncover the wellspring of inspiration that exists in the world around us, often overlooked in the hustle and bustle of daily life.

Inspiration is the lifeblood of human creativity and innovation. It fuels our passions, drives our ambitions, and propels us toward new horizons of possibility. Yet, in our fast-paced, technology-driven world, we often find ourselves searching for inspiration in grand gestures and extraordinary experiences, neglecting the wealth of inspiration that lies in the seemingly mundane aspects of our everyday lives. This book challenges that notion, inviting readers to rediscover the magic in the ordinary and tap into the boundless creative potential that surrounds us at every moment.

Drawing from a diverse range of disciplines including psychology, neuroscience, art, literature, and nature studies, "Everyday Sparks" offers a fresh perspective on the nature of inspiration and its profound impact on personal growth and societal progress. By exploring the intricate relationship between our environment, our senses, and our creative faculties, this book unveils the hidden connections that can spark revolutionary ideas and transformative insights.

What sets "Everyday Sparks" apart is its practical approach to cultivating inspiration in daily life. Rather than presenting inspiration as an elusive, lightning-bolt moment reserved for the gifted few, this book demystifies the process of finding and nurturing creative sparks. Through a combination of scientific research, real-life case studies, and hands-on exercises, readers will learn to develop a more observant mindset, sharpen their perceptual skills, and create personal rituals that invite inspiration into their lives on a regular basis.

As we delve into the pages of "Everyday Sparks," several key themes emerge that form the foundation of our exploration. First, we examine the nature of inspiration itself, unraveling the psychological and neurological processes that underpin those "aha" moments that can change the course of our lives. By understanding the mechanics of inspiration, we can learn to cultivate it more intentionally and harness its power to drive personal and professional growth.

Second, we explore the concept of "awakening to the ordinary," a fundamental shift in perspective that allows us to see the extraordinary potential in everyday experiences. Through various techniques and exercises, readers will learn to develop a more observant mindset, attuning themselves to the subtle details and hidden connections that often go unnoticed. This heightened awareness not only enriches our daily experiences but also opens up new avenues for creative thinking and problem-solving.

Third, we delve into the myriad sources of inspiration that surround us in our daily lives. From the intricate patterns of nature to the vibrant tapestry of human connections, from the visual feast of art and architecture to the emotive power of music and literature, we explore how different sensory experiences can spark creativity and innovation. Readers will discover techniques for tapping into these diverse wellsprings of inspiration, learning to draw creative fuel from both their immediate environment and the vast digital landscape at their fingertips.

Fourth, we address the common obstacles that can block the flow of inspiration, such as creative blocks, self-doubt, and the pressures of daily life. By identifying these barriers and providing strategies to overcome them, "Everyday Sparks" equips readers with the tools they need to maintain a consistent flow of creativity and inspiration, even in the face of challenges.

Finally, we explore the concept of "cultivating an inspired life," showing readers how to integrate inspiration-seeking practices into their daily routines and create a lifestyle that nurtures creativity and personal growth. This holistic approach encourages readers not only to seek inspiration for themselves but also to become sources of inspiration for others, creating a ripple effect of creativity and positive change in their communities and beyond.

"Everyday Sparks" is written for anyone who seeks to infuse their life with greater creativity, purpose, and joy. Whether you're an artist looking to break through a creative block, an entrepreneur searching for innovative solutions, a professional aiming to bring fresh energy to your work, or simply an individual yearning to live a more inspired and fulfilling life, this book offers valuable insights and practical tools to help you achieve your goals.

By reading "Everyday Sparks," you'll gain a new appreciation for the world around you and develop the skills to transform ordinary moments into extraordinary opportunities for growth and creativity. You'll learn to see with new eyes, listen with new ears, and engage with your environment in ways that continuously fuel your imagination and drive your personal evolution. More than just a guide to finding inspiration, this book is a roadmap to living an inspired life – one where every day holds the potential for discovery, growth, and meaningful change.

As you turn the pages of "Everyday Sparks," prepare to embark on a transformative journey that will reshape your perception of the world and your place within it. You'll discover that inspiration isn't a rare commodity reserved for special occasions, but a constant presence waiting to be acknowledged and embraced. With each chapter, you'll gain new tools and perspectives that will empower you to tap into this endless wellspring of creativity and inspiration.

You'll learn how to transform your daily commute into a treasure hunt for visual inspiration, turning mundane street scenes into catalysts for creative breakthroughs. You'll discover how to extract profound insights from casual conversations, recognizing the spark of genius that can arise from the most unexpected exchanges. You'll explore techniques for using literature as a launching pad for your own ideas, learning to read not just for information but for inspiration.

As you progress through the book, you'll develop a keener sense of observation, noticing the intricate patterns in nature that have inspired countless innovations throughout human history. You'll learn to listen more deeply to the world around you, recognizing how the rhythm of raindrops or the buzz of a busy café can spark new ideas and creative solutions. You'll explore the digital realm with fresh eyes, learning to curate online experiences that nourish your creativity rather than deplete it.

But "Everyday Sparks" offers more than just techniques for finding inspiration; it provides a framework for integrating these practices into your daily life in a sustainable way. You'll learn how to create personal rituals that invite inspiration, how to overcome creative blocks when they arise, and how to maintain motivation even in the face of setbacks. By the end of the book, you'll have developed a comprehensive toolkit for living a more inspired and creative life.

Moreover, you'll gain a deeper understanding of the vital role that inspiration plays in personal growth, innovation, and societal progress. You'll see how seemingly small moments of inspiration have led to world-changing inventions, groundbreaking artistic movements, and profound shifts in human understanding. This broader perspective will help you appreciate the value of your own creative insights, no matter how small they may seem at first.

Perhaps most importantly, "Everyday Sparks" will challenge you to become not just a seeker of inspiration, but a source of it as well. As you learn to recognize and cultivate the sparks of creativity in your own life, you'll naturally begin to share this energy with others. Whether through your work, your relationships, or your engagement with your community, you'll become a catalyst for positive change, spreading the ripples of inspiration far beyond your immediate sphere.

As we stand on the brink of a new chapter in human history, faced with unprecedented challenges and opportunities, the ability to find inspiration in the everyday has never been more crucial. The solutions to our most pressing problems, the innovations that will shape our future, and the ideas that will define our culture may well arise not from grand initiatives or elaborate plans, but from a moment of insight sparked by a common experience viewed through an inspired lens.

So, as you prepare to dive into the pages of "Everyday Sparks," open your mind to the possibilities that surround you. Let go of preconceived notions about where inspiration comes from or what it should look like. Instead, approach each page with curiosity and openness, ready to discover the extraordinary potential hidden within the ordinary moments of your life.

Remember, every great idea, every transformative innovation, every life-changing realization began with a single spark. As you learn to recognize and nurture these sparks in your daily life, you'll not only enrich your own experience but contribute to the collective creativity and progress of our world. The journey to a more inspired life begins with a single step – or in this case, a single page. Are you ready to ignite your creativity and discover the everyday sparks that can illuminate your path to a more inspired, fulfilling life? Let's begin.

Chapter 1: The Nature of Inspiration

As we embark on this journey to explore the wellsprings of creativity that surround us, it is fitting to begin by examining the very essence of inspiration itself. Inspiration, that elusive spark that ignites our imagination and propels us towards new horizons, is a fundamental force in human creativity and innovation. It is the catalyst that transforms ordinary moments into extraordinary revelations, and mundane observations into groundbreaking ideas.

Defining inspiration is no simple task, as it encompasses a wide range of experiences and emotions. At its core, inspiration can be understood as a sudden and often profound realization or idea that stimulates us to action or creation. It is that moment when disparate thoughts coalesce into a coherent vision, or when an external stimulus triggers an internal epiphany. The acclaimed author Elizabeth Gilbert describes inspiration as "ideas being alive, and ideas searching for available and willing human partners." This personification of inspiration as an active force seeking expression through human vessels captures the mysterious and often unpredictable nature of inspirational moments.

The role of inspiration in human creativity cannot be overstated. Throughout history, countless innovations, artistic masterpieces, and scientific breakthroughs have been attributed to moments of inspiration. From Archimedes' famous "Eureka!" moment in his bathtub to Paul McCartney dreaming the melody of "Yesterday," inspiration has been the driving force behind some of humanity's greatest achievements. It serves as the bridge between the known and the unknown, allowing us to transcend our current limitations and explore new possibilities.

Inspiration acts as a catalyst for creative thinking, problem-solving, and personal growth. When inspired, we often find ourselves capable of feats we previously thought impossible. Our minds become more flexible, our perception sharpens, and our ability to make connections between seemingly unrelated concepts intensifies. This heightened state of cognitive function is not merely a subjective experience but has been observed and studied by psychologists and neuroscientists.

The psychology behind inspirational moments is a fascinating area of study that sheds light on the inner workings of the creative mind. Research has shown that inspiration is often characterized by three main components: evocation, transcendence, and motivation. Evocation refers to the spontaneous nature of inspiration, how it seems to arise unbidden from external stimuli or internal reflection. Transcendence speaks to the way inspiration elevates us beyond our ordinary concerns and limitations, providing a glimpse of greater possibilities. Motivation is the driving force that compels us to act on our inspiration, to bring our ideas into reality.

Neuroscientific studies have begun to unravel the brain mechanisms underlying inspirational experiences. During moments of inspiration, researchers have observed increased activity in the default mode network of the brain, a region associated with introspection and self-referential thinking. This suggests that inspiration often emerges when we allow our minds to wander and make unexpected connections. Additionally, the release of dopamine during inspirational experiences contributes to the sense of pleasure and motivation that accompanies these moments.

The impact of inspiration on personal growth and innovation is profound and far-reaching. On a personal level, inspiration can be a powerful motivator for self-improvement and the pursuit of goals. When we are inspired, we often feel a renewed sense of purpose and a heightened belief in our own capabilities. This boost in self-efficacy can lead to increased perseverance in the face of challenges and a greater willingness to take risks and explore new opportunities.

In the realm of innovation, inspiration is often the spark that ignites the fire of progress. Many of the world's most revolutionary inventions and discoveries have been attributed to moments of inspiration. Take, for example, the story of Alexander Fleming's discovery of penicillin. Fleming's inspiring moment came when he noticed that mold contaminating one of his petri dishes had created a bacteria-free circle around itself. This chance observation, combined with Fleming's prepared mind and willingness to explore the unexpected, led to one of the most significant medical breakthroughs of the 20th century.

Inspiration also plays a crucial role in fostering a culture of innovation within organizations and societies. When individuals and groups are encouraged to seek out and act upon their inspirations, it creates an environment ripe for creative problem-solving and groundbreaking ideas. Companies like Google and 3M have famously implemented policies that allow employees dedicated time to pursue their own inspirations and passion projects, recognizing the potential for these moments of creativity to lead to valuable innovations.

The relationship between inspiration and hard work is a complex one. While moments of inspiration can feel effortless and spontaneous, they often emerge from a foundation of knowledge, experience, and preparation. As Louis Pasteur famously said, "Chance favors the prepared mind." This suggests that while we cannot force inspiration to occur, we can create conditions that make us more receptive to it. Cultivating expertise in our chosen fields, exposing ourselves to diverse experiences and ideas, and maintaining an open and curious mindset all contribute to our ability to recognize and capitalize on inspirational moments when they arise.

It's important to note that inspiration, while powerful, is not a substitute for dedication and perseverance. Many people mistakenly believe that truly inspired work should flow effortlessly, without struggle or revision. In reality, even the most inspired ideas often require significant refinement and hard work to bring to fruition. The Wright brothers' inspiration to create a flying machine was just the beginning of years of experimentation, failure, and persistence before they achieved their goal.

Understanding the nature of inspiration also involves recognizing its ephemeral quality. Inspirational moments can be fleeting, and the intensity of the initial spark often fades quickly. This is why it's crucial to develop strategies for capturing and nurturing our inspirations. Keeping a notebook or digital record of ideas, creating rough sketches or prototypes, and discussing concepts with others can all help to preserve and develop inspirational thoughts before they slip away.

The democratization of inspiration in the modern age is another fascinating aspect to consider. With the advent of the internet and social media, we now have unprecedented access to a vast array of potentially inspiring content and ideas from around the world. This global interconnectedness has the potential to spark inspiration across cultural and geographical boundaries, leading to new forms of collaboration and innovation. However, it also presents challenges in terms of information overload and the need to cultivate discernment in our inspirational sources.

As we delve deeper into the nature of inspiration, it becomes clear that it is not merely a passive experience that happens to us, but an active process that we can cultivate and nurture. By understanding the psychological and neurological underpinnings of inspirational moments, we can begin to create environments and practices that increase our receptivity to inspiration. This might involve setting aside time for reflection and daydreaming, exposing ourselves to new experiences and perspectives, or engaging in activities that challenge our assumptions and spark our curiosity.

The role of emotions in the inspirational process is another crucial aspect to explore. Inspiration is often accompanied by positive emotions such as excitement, awe, and a sense of possibility. These emotions not only make the experience of inspiration enjoyable but also play a functional role in motivating us to act on our ideas. Positive emotions have been shown to broaden our attention and thought-action repertoires, making us more open to new experiences and ideas – a state highly conducive to inspiration and creativity.

However, it's important to recognize that inspiration can also arise from challenging or even negative experiences. Many artists and innovators have found profound inspiration in moments of struggle, loss, or adversity. The key lies in our ability to transmute these experiences into something meaningful and constructive. This transformative power of inspiration highlights its potential not just as a catalyst for creativity, but as a means of personal growth and resilience.

As we conclude our exploration of the nature of inspiration, we stand on the threshold of a journey that will take us through the myriad ways in which inspiration manifests in our everyday lives. From the quiet whispers of nature to the bustling energy of human connections, from the visual feast of art and design to the rhythmic pulse of music and sound, inspiration awaits us in every corner of our existence. In the chapters that follow, we will delve into these various realms of inspiration, uncovering techniques and strategies for awakening our senses to the extraordinary possibilities that lie hidden within the ordinary moments of our lives.

Our next step will be to examine how we can awaken to the ordinary, recognizing the extraordinary potential that exists in our everyday experiences. By developing a more observant mindset and honing our ability to find wonder in the mundane, we open ourselves to a world brimming with inspirational opportunities. As we transition into this exploration of the ordinary, let us carry with us the understanding that inspiration is not a rare and elusive phenomenon, but a constant companion waiting to be acknowledged and embraced.

Chapter 2: Awakening to the Ordinary

As we transition from our exploration of the nature of inspiration in the previous chapter, we now turn our attention to the often-overlooked wellspring of creativity that surrounds us daily. In Chapter 2, we delve into the art of awakening to the ordinary, discovering how the seemingly mundane aspects of our lives can become rich sources of inspiration and catalysts for personal growth and innovation.

Recognizing the extraordinary in everyday experiences is a skill that can be cultivated with practice and intention. Our daily lives are filled with moments, objects, and interactions that we often overlook or take for granted. Yet, these very elements can serve as powerful triggers for creative thought and inspiration if we learn to perceive them with fresh eyes and an open mind.

Consider the humble coffee mug sitting on your desk. At first glance, it might seem unremarkable – a simple vessel for your morning brew. However, if we pause to truly observe it, we might notice the interplay of light and shadow on its curved surface, the subtle variations in color and texture, or the way its shape fits perfectly in our hands. This everyday object suddenly becomes a study in design, functionality, and aesthetics. It might inspire thoughts about the cultural significance of shared beverages, the engineering principles behind heat retention, or the artistry involved in pottery making.

The renowned artist Georgia O'Keeffe once said, "When you take a flower in your hand and really look at it, it's your world for the moment. I want to give that world to someone else." This quote encapsulates the essence of finding inspiration in the ordinary. By truly engaging with the world around us, we can transform even the most common objects or experiences into sources of wonder and creativity.

Developing a more observant mindset is crucial in this process of awakening to the ordinary. It requires us to slow down, to be present in the moment, and to engage our senses fully. This heightened state of awareness allows us to notice details, patterns, and connections that we might otherwise miss in our rush through daily life.

One technique for cultivating this observant mindset is the practice of mindful walking. Instead of hurrying from point A to point B with your mind preoccupied with tasks and worries, try taking a leisurely stroll with the sole purpose of observing your surroundings. Pay attention to the rhythm of your footsteps, the texture of the ground beneath your feet, the play of light and shadow on buildings and trees. Listen to the cacophony of urban sounds or the subtle whispers of nature. Smell the air, noting how scents change as you move through different areas.

This simple exercise can transform an ordinary walk into a rich sensory experience, providing a wealth of inspiration for creative endeavors. A street musician's melody might spark an idea for a composition, the pattern of cracks in the sidewalk could inspire a new textile design, or an overheard snippet of conversation might become the seed of a short story.

Another powerful technique for recognizing the extraordinary in the everyday is the practice of journaling. Set aside time each day to record your observations, thoughts, and experiences. Don't censor yourself or worry about creating polished prose – the goal is to capture the raw material of your daily life. You might describe an interesting interaction you had with a stranger, sketch a peculiar cloud formation you noticed, or jot down a metaphor that occurred to you while doing the dishes.

Over time, this journal becomes a treasure trove of inspiration, filled with the unique details and perspectives of your life. Reviewing your entries can reveal patterns, themes, and ideas that you might not have noticed in the moment, providing fuel for creative projects or personal growth.

The power of finding inspiration in the commonplace is beautifully illustrated by the case of James Dyson, the inventor of the bagless vacuum cleaner. Dyson's revolutionary idea came not from a high-tech laboratory or a brainstorming session, but from an everyday frustration with his own vacuum cleaner. He noticed how the bag would clog and lose suction, reducing the cleaner's efficiency. This ordinary observation led him to experiment with cyclonic separation, a principle he had seen at work in a local sawmill. By applying this industrial concept to a household appliance, Dyson created a product that transformed the vacuum cleaner industry.

Similarly, the invention of Post-it notes by Dr. Spencer Silver at 3M came from a seeming failure in developing a super-strong adhesive. Instead of discarding the weak, pressure-sensitive adhesive he accidentally created, Silver recognized its unique properties. It wasn't until his colleague Art Fry applied this adhesive to bookmarks that kept falling out of his hymnal that the full potential of the invention was realized. This everyday problem of loose bookmarks led to the creation of one of the most ubiquitous office supplies in the world.

These examples demonstrate how paying attention to everyday problems, frustrations, or quirks can lead to groundbreaking innovations. They remind us that inspiration doesn't always come in dramatic flashes or grand epiphanies, but often emerges from a keen observation of the world around us and a willingness to question the status quo.

The artist Andy Warhol famously elevated everyday objects to the status of high art, challenging viewers to see the beauty and significance in soup cans, Brillo boxes, and other consumer goods. His work serves as a powerful reminder that inspiration can be found in the most unexpected places, and that our perception shapes what we consider ordinary or extraordinary.

To further develop your ability to find inspiration in the mundane, try the "Five Senses" exercise. Choose an everyday object or experience and spend five minutes exploring it with each of your senses. For example, if you choose an apple, start by looking at it closely, noting its color, shape, and any unique markings. Then close your eyes and feel its texture, weight, and temperature. Smell it, listening to the sound it makes when you tap or bite into it, and finally, taste it mindfully. This deep sensory exploration can reveal new aspects of even the most familiar objects, sparking creative associations and ideas.

Another technique for awakening to the ordinary is to practice "defamiliarization" – a concept introduced by Russian formalist Viktor Shklovsky. This involves looking at familiar objects or situations as if you're encountering them for the first time. Imagine you're an alien visiting Earth, or a time traveler from the past, and describe everyday scenes or objects from this fresh perspective. This exercise can help break through habitual patterns of perception and reveal the inherent strangeness and wonder of the world around us.

The photographer Dorothea Lange once said, "The camera is an instrument that teaches people how to see without a camera." This insight applies not just to photography but to all forms of creative expression. By cultivating a more observant mindset, we train ourselves to see the world more deeply and clearly, even when we're not actively creating.

As we conclude this chapter on awakening to the ordinary, it's important to remember that inspiration is not something that happens to us passively, but a skill we can actively cultivate. By learning to recognize the extraordinary in everyday experiences, we open ourselves to a constant stream of creative possibilities. We transform our daily lives from a series of mundane routines into a rich tapestry of potential inspiration.

In the next chapter, we'll explore how nature, one of the most accessible and abundant sources of inspiration, can serve as a powerful muse for creativity and innovation. We'll discover techniques for connecting with the natural world, even in urban environments, and examine how nature-inspired innovations have shaped human progress throughout history.

Chapter 3: Nature's Muse

As we transition from awakening to the ordinary, we now turn our attention to one of the most profound and inexhaustible sources of inspiration: the natural world. Nature has been a wellspring of creativity, innovation, and wonder for countless generations, offering a rich tapestry of experiences that can ignite the spark of inspiration within us. In this chapter, we will delve into the myriad ways in which the natural world can serve as our muse, exploring techniques for connecting with nature even in urban environments, and examining how nature-inspired innovations have shaped human progress throughout history.

The power of nature to inspire has been recognized by artists, scientists, and thinkers for millennia. From the intricate patterns of a snowflake to the awe-inspiring expanse of a starry night sky, the natural world offers an endless array of wonders that can captivate our imagination and stimulate our creativity. As the renowned naturalist John Muir once said, "In every walk with nature, one receives far more than he seeks." This sentiment encapsulates the profound impact that immersing ourselves in nature can have on our creative spirit and overall well-being.

One of the most striking aspects of nature as a source of inspiration is its ability to evoke a sense of awe and wonder. When we stand before a majestic mountain range or witness the delicate dance of a butterfly, we are often struck by a feeling of smallness in the face of something much greater than ourselves. This experience of awe can be transformative, shifting our perspective and opening our minds to new possibilities. Research has shown that experiences of awe can enhance creative thinking and problem-solving abilities, making nature an invaluable resource for those seeking to cultivate their creative potential.

Moreover, the natural world offers a repository of solutions to complex problems that have been refined over millions of years of evolution. This concept, known as biomimicry, has led to countless innovations across various fields, from engineering to medicine. By observing and learning from nature's ingenious designs, we can unlock new approaches to human challenges and spark revolutionary ideas. For instance, the invention of Velcro was inspired by the way burrs cling to animal fur, while the streamlined shape of bullet trains in Japan was modeled after the aerodynamic beak of the kingfisher bird.

To truly harness the inspirational power of nature, we must cultivate a deep connection with the natural world. This connection begins with mindful observation and presence. When we take the time to truly see, hear, smell, and feel our natural surroundings, we open ourselves to a wealth of sensory experiences that can stimulate our creativity. The rustling of leaves in the wind, the intricate patterns of bark on a tree trunk, or the vibrant colors of a sunset can all serve as catalysts for new ideas and fresh perspectives.

One effective technique for deepening our connection with nature is the practice of "forest bathing" or shinrin-yoku, which originated in Japan. This practice involves immersing oneself in a forest environment, using all five senses to engage with the natural surroundings. Studies have shown that forest bathing can reduce stress, improve mood, and enhance cognitive function – all of which are conducive to creative thinking and inspiration. By incorporating regular nature walks or forest bathing sessions into our routines, we can tap into a constant source of renewal and inspiration.

For those living in urban environments, connecting with nature may seem challenging at first glance. However, nature can be found in even the most concrete-laden cities if we know where to look. Urban parks, community gardens, and even small patches of green space can serve as oases of natural inspiration in the midst of bustling city life. The key is to approach these spaces with an open and curious mind, ready to discover the hidden wonders they contain.

In addition to seeking out green spaces, urban dwellers can bring nature into their daily lives in various ways. Keeping houseplants, creating a small herb garden on a windowsill, or even simply observing the changing patterns of clouds in the sky can help maintain a connection to the natural world. As the poet Mary Oliver wrote, "Attention is the beginning of devotion." By cultivating attention to the natural elements around us, no matter how small, we can nurture our capacity for inspiration and wonder.

The relationship between humans and nature has also been a rich source of inspiration for artists throughout history. From the cave paintings of Lascaux to the nature-inspired works of contemporary eco-artists, the natural world has consistently served as a muse for creative expression. By studying these artworks and the artists who created them, we can gain insight into different ways of perceiving and interpreting the natural world, further expanding our own capacity for nature-inspired creativity.

One particularly powerful way to draw inspiration from nature is through the practice of biomimicry. This approach involves studying nature's time-tested patterns and strategies and applying them to solve human problems. For example, the structure of sharkskin has inspired the development of swimsuits that reduce drag in the water, while the self-cleaning properties of lotus leaves have led to the creation of water-repellent coatings for buildings and vehicles. By adopting a biomimetic mindset, we can train ourselves to see potential solutions and innovations in every aspect of the natural world around us.

The inspirational power of nature extends beyond the visual realm. The sounds of nature, from the gentle lapping of waves on a shore to the melodious songs of birds, can also serve as powerful catalysts for creativity. Many composers, including Beethoven and Debussy, have drawn inspiration from natural soundscapes in their music. By taking the time to listen deeply to the natural world, we can attune ourselves to new rhythms and harmonies that can inform our own creative endeavors.

Similarly, the scents and tastes associated with nature can evoke powerful emotions and memories that can fuel our creative processes. The earthy smell of soil after rain, the crisp scent of pine needles, or the tang of wild berries can all trigger associations and ideas that lead to new inspirations. By engaging all our senses in our exploration of nature, we can create a richer, more multifaceted wellspring of creative inspiration.

One of the most profound ways in which nature inspires is through its cycles and processes. The changing of seasons, the ebb and flow of tides, and the growth cycles of plants all offer metaphors and models for understanding change, renewal, and transformation in our own lives and creative processes. By observing and reflecting on these natural cycles, we can gain insights into the rhythms of creativity and find comfort in the natural ebb and flow of inspiration.

The concept of biomimicry extends beyond individual inventions to entire systems and processes. For instance, the principles of circular economy, which aims to eliminate waste and maximize resource use, are inspired by the closed-loop systems found in nature where nothing is wasted. By studying ecosystem dynamics, we can find inspiration for more sustainable and efficient ways of organizing our societies and economies.

Moreover, nature provides us with countless examples of resilience and adaptability – qualities that are essential for any creative endeavor. From the way trees bend in strong winds to avoid breaking, to the remarkable ability of certain animals to regenerate lost limbs, nature offers lessons in flexibility and perseverance that we can apply to our own creative challenges. By cultivating a nature-inspired resilience, we can learn to view obstacles as opportunities for growth and innovation.

The inspirational power of nature is not limited to its physical manifestations. The concepts and principles underlying natural phenomena can also spark profound insights and ideas. For example, the theory of evolution has inspired innovations far beyond the field of biology, influencing areas such as computer science, economics, and even music composition. By delving into the fundamental principles that govern the natural world, we can uncover new paradigms and approaches that can revolutionize our thinking across various disciplines.

As we continue to face global challenges such as climate change and biodiversity loss, drawing inspiration from nature becomes not just a source of creativity, but a necessity for our survival and flourishing. By reconnecting with the natural world and learning from its wisdom, we can find innovative solutions to pressing problems and chart a more sustainable course for our future.

In conclusion, nature serves as an inexhaustible wellspring of inspiration, offering countless opportunities for wonder, learning, and creative growth. By cultivating a deep connection with the natural world, we open ourselves to a universe of possibilities that can enrich our lives and fuel our creative endeavors. As we move forward in our exploration of everyday sparks of inspiration, let us carry with us the lessons and wonders of nature, allowing them to inform and enhance our perception of the world around us. In the next chapter, we will delve into the art of seeing, exploring how we can develop a keen eye for visual inspiration in our daily lives.

Chapter 4: The Art of Seeing

As we transition from exploring the natural world as a source of inspiration, we now turn our attention to the visual realm and the art of seeing. This chapter delves into the profound impact that developing a keen eye for visual inspiration can have on our creative processes and overall perception of the world around us.

The Art of Seeing

Developing a keen eye for visual inspiration is a skill that can transform the way we interact with our environment. It's not merely about looking at things; it's about truly seeing them, understanding their essence, and allowing them to spark our creativity. This process begins with an acknowledgment that inspiration can be found in the most unexpected places, from the intricate patterns on a leaf to the bold lines of a skyscraper.

To cultivate this skill, one must first learn to slow down and observe. In our fast-paced world, we often rush through our days, barely noticing the visual feast that surrounds us. By taking the time to pause and really look at our surroundings, we open ourselves up to a world of inspiration. This practice of mindful observation can be as simple as spending a few minutes each day focusing on a single object, noting its colors, textures, and shapes.

The renowned artist Georgia O'Keeffe once said, "Nobody sees a flower - really - it is so small it takes time - we haven't time - and to see takes time, like to have a friend takes time." This quote encapsulates the essence of developing a keen eye. It's about dedicating time and attention to the act of seeing, allowing ourselves to be fully present in the moment and open to the inspiration that may arise.

As we hone our observational skills, we begin to notice details that we might have previously overlooked. The way light falls across a room, creating shadows and highlights, can become a source of inspiration for a painting or a photograph. The juxtaposition of colors in a city street scene might spark an idea for a new color palette in a design project. Even the most mundane objects can take on new significance when viewed with fresh eyes.

This heightened awareness extends beyond the visual arts. Writers, for instance, can find inspiration in the body language of people they observe, using these visual cues to inform their character descriptions. Architects might draw inspiration from the organic forms found in nature, incorporating these shapes into their building designs. The ability to see deeply and draw inspiration from visual stimuli can enhance creativity across all disciplines.

One effective technique for developing this skill is to engage in regular sketching or photography sessions. These practices force us to look closely at our subjects, considering their forms, proportions, and relationships to their surroundings. Even for those who don't consider themselves artists, the act of attempting to capture what they see can sharpen their observational skills and open new avenues for inspiration.

Another powerful tool for honing our visual perception is the study of art history and theory. By examining the works of master artists and understanding the principles of design, we can train our eyes to recognize beauty and meaning in a wide range of visual stimuli. This knowledge provides a framework for analyzing and appreciating the visual world around us, allowing us to draw inspiration from both classical masterpieces and contemporary installations.

The field of architecture offers a particularly rich source of visual inspiration. Buildings are more than just functional structures; they are physical manifestations of ideas, cultural values, and artistic expression. By observing architectural designs, we can gain insights into the interplay of form and function, the use of space and light, and the ways in which human needs and aesthetic considerations can be balanced.

Frank Lloyd Wright, one of the most influential architects of the 20th century, was known for his ability to draw inspiration from nature and translate it into his designs. He once stated, "Study nature, love nature, stay close to nature. It will never fail you." This philosophy is evident in his organic architecture, which sought to create harmony between human habitation and the natural environment. By studying Wright's work and approach, we can learn to see the potential for inspiration in the relationship between built structures and their surroundings.

> 1. In the realm of design, developing a keen eye for visual inspiration is crucial. Designers must be able to identify trends, understand visual hierarchies, and recognize effective use of color, typography, and imagery. This requires constant observation and analysis of the designed world around us, from product packaging to user interfaces.

One technique for enhancing visual perception in design is to create mood boards or visual journals. These collections of images, color swatches, textures, and other visual elements can serve as a repository of inspiration, helping designers to identify patterns and themes that resonate with them. By regularly adding to and reviewing these collections, designers can train their eyes to spot potential sources of inspiration in their daily lives.

The digital age has provided us with unprecedented access to visual stimuli from around the world. Social media platforms like Instagram and Pinterest offer endless streams of images that can serve as sources of inspiration. However, it's important to approach these digital resources mindfully, using them as tools to enhance our real-world observations rather than replacing them entirely.

One effective exercise for enhancing visual perception and creativity is the practice of "visual meditation." This involves selecting a single object or scene and spending an extended period of time observing it in detail. As you focus on the subject, allow your mind to wander and make connections. What does the object remind you of? What emotions does it evoke? How might it be transformed or incorporated into a creative project? This exercise can help to break down the barriers between observation and imagination, allowing for more fluid and inspired thinking.

Another valuable technique is to engage in regular "inspiration walks." These can be conducted in any environment, from bustling city streets to quiet natural settings. The key is to approach the walk with an open mind and a deliberate focus on visual details. Take note of color combinations, textures, patterns, and forms that catch your eye. Consider how these elements might be applied in your own creative work.

It's also important to recognize that developing a keen eye for visual inspiration is not just about looking outward, but also about cultivating our inner vision. Our memories, dreams, and imaginations are rich sources of visual inspiration that we can tap into. By practicing visualization techniques and keeping a dream journal, we can strengthen our ability to generate and manipulate mental images, enhancing our overall visual creativity.

The process of developing a keen eye for visual inspiration is ongoing and deeply personal. What sparks inspiration for one person may not resonate with another. It's important to trust our own instincts and allow ourselves to be drawn to the visual elements that speak to us on a deeper level. As we continue to refine our observational skills and expand our visual vocabulary, we'll find that inspiration becomes more readily available to us in our everyday lives.

As we conclude this exploration of the art of seeing, it's clear that developing a keen eye for visual inspiration is a transformative process that can enrich our creative pursuits and our daily experiences. By learning to truly see the world around us, we open ourselves up to a constant stream of inspiration that can fuel our creativity and spark new ideas.

As we move forward, we'll explore how this heightened visual awareness can be complemented by the power of human connections. The next chapter will delve into the ways in which our relationships and interactions with others can serve as rich sources of inspiration, adding another dimension to our creative toolkit.

Chapter 5: The Power of Human Connections

As we transition from exploring the visual world of inspiration, we now turn our attention to the rich tapestry of human connections and their profound impact on our creative journey. Chapter 5: The Power of Human Connections delves into the intricate ways in which our interactions with others can spark inspiration and fuel our creative pursuits.

Human connections have long been recognized as a wellspring of inspiration, driving innovation, artistic expression, and personal growth. The simple act of engaging with another person can open up new perspectives, challenge our assumptions, and ignite sparks of creativity that we may never have discovered on our own. As the renowned psychologist Mihaly Csikszentmihalyi once observed, "Creativity is not the product of individuals working in isolation, but rather of people interacting within a sociocultural context."

One of the most potent sources of inspiration through human connections is the exchange of ideas. When we engage in meaningful conversations with others, we expose ourselves to diverse viewpoints, experiences, and knowledge bases. This cross-pollination of thoughts can lead to unexpected insights and novel combinations of ideas. Consider the historic coffeehouses of 17th and 18th century Europe, where intellectuals, artists, and thinkers would gather to discuss philosophy, politics, and the arts. These vibrant social hubs became crucibles of creativity, fostering movements like the Enlightenment and nurturing the talents of figures such as Voltaire, Diderot, and Benjamin Franklin.

In our modern world, the opportunities for such intellectually stimulating encounters have expanded beyond physical spaces. Online forums, social media platforms, and virtual meetups now allow us to connect with individuals from diverse backgrounds and cultures, broadening our horizons and exposing us to a global tapestry of ideas. However, it's important to note that the quality of these interactions matters more than their quantity. Shallow exchanges or echo chambers of like-minded individuals are less likely to spark true inspiration than deep, authentic conversations that challenge our preconceptions and push us to think in new ways.

The power of human connections in sparking inspiration is not limited to intellectual discourse. Emotional connections and shared experiences can also be profound sources of creative energy. The support and encouragement of friends, family, or mentors can provide the confidence and motivation needed to pursue ambitious creative endeavors. Similarly, witnessing the passion and dedication of others can be deeply inspiring, spurring us to push our own boundaries and strive for excellence in our chosen fields.

Consider the story of the Impressionist movement in art. The group of artists who would come to revolutionize painting in the late 19th century initially found inspiration and support in each other's company. Claude Monet, Pierre-Auguste Renoir, Alfred Sisley, and Frédéric Bazille often painted together en plein air, sharing techniques, critiquing each other's work, and collectively developing the style that would come to define Impressionism. Their camaraderie and shared vision not only inspired their individual works but also gave them the courage to challenge the artistic conventions of their time.

The inspiration derived from human connections can also stem from unexpected sources. Sometimes, a chance encounter with a stranger or a brief interaction with someone from a completely different walk of life can provide the spark that ignites a new idea or perspective. These serendipitous moments of connection remind us of the vast potential for inspiration that exists in the world around us, if only we remain open to it.

To harness the power of human connections for inspiration, it's essential to cultivate the skills of meaningful conversation and active listening. Engaging in deep, authentic dialogue requires more than simply waiting for your turn to speak. It involves truly hearing what others are saying, seeking to understand their perspectives, and being willing to question your own assumptions. As the philosopher Martin Buber famously articulated, true dialogue occurs in the space between people, in what he called the "I-Thou" relationship, where both parties are fully present and open to being changed by the encounter.

Developing active listening skills is crucial for tapping into the inspirational potential of human connections. This involves not only hearing the words being spoken but also paying attention to non-verbal cues, emotional undertones, and the broader context of the conversation. By fully immersing ourselves in the act of listening, we open ourselves up to new ideas and perspectives that might otherwise pass us by.

One effective technique for enhancing active listening is the practice of reflective listening. This involves paraphrasing or summarizing what the other person has said to ensure understanding and demonstrate engagement. By doing so, we not only show respect for the speaker but also give ourselves the opportunity to process and internalize the information more deeply, potentially uncovering inspirational insights in the process.

Another powerful tool for fostering inspirational connections is the art of asking thoughtful questions. By posing open-ended, probing questions, we can encourage others to delve deeper into their thoughts and experiences, potentially unearthing ideas and insights that even they were not fully aware of. This process of collaborative exploration can be mutually inspiring, leading to new avenues of thought and creativity for both parties.

The power of human connections in sparking inspiration is perhaps most evident in the realm of collaboration. When individuals with diverse skills, perspectives, and experiences come together to work towards a common goal, the potential for transformative ideas and innovations is immense. The history of human progress is replete with examples of groundbreaking collaborations that have changed the course of science, art, and society.

One such example is the partnership between James Watson and Francis Crick, which led to the discovery of the structure of DNA. Watson, a biologist, and Crick, a physicist, brought complementary skills and knowledge to their collaboration. Their different backgrounds allowed them to approach the problem from unique angles, ultimately leading to their revolutionary insight into the double helix structure of DNA. This discovery not only earned them a Nobel Prize but also laid the foundation for modern genetics and biotechnology.

In the world of technology, the collaboration between Steve Jobs and Steve Wozniak in founding Apple Computer is another testament to the power of human connections in fostering innovation. Jobs' visionary marketing acumen and design sensibility combined with Wozniak's technical brilliance to create products that would revolutionize personal computing and consumer electronics. Their partnership demonstrates how the synergy between different skill sets and perspectives can lead to truly transformative innovations.

Collaborations need not always be formal partnerships to be inspirational. Sometimes, casual brainstorming sessions or impromptu discussions can lead to unexpected breakthroughs. The key is to create an environment where ideas can flow freely, and diverse perspectives are welcomed and valued. This might involve organizing regular meetups with colleagues or friends from different fields, participating in interdisciplinary workshops, or simply being open to spontaneous conversations with new acquaintances.

While the power of human connections in sparking inspiration is undeniable, it's important to recognize that not all interactions will be equally inspirational. Some may even be draining or discouraging. Learning to navigate these different types of connections and cultivating relationships that are truly nourishing to our creative spirits is an important skill in itself.

One way to foster more inspirational connections is to seek out individuals who share our passions or who are pursuing similar creative goals. This might involve joining professional associations, attending industry conferences, or participating in online communities focused on our areas of interest. By surrounding ourselves with like-minded individuals, we create opportunities for mutual inspiration and support.

However, it's equally important to maintain connections with people from diverse backgrounds and fields. Cross-pollination of ideas from different domains can often lead to the most unexpected and innovative inspirations. As Steve Jobs famously said, "Creativity is just connecting things. When you ask creative people how they did something, they feel a little guilty because they didn't really do it, they just saw something. It seemed obvious to them after a while."

In our increasingly digital world, it's crucial to strike a balance between online and offline connections. While digital platforms offer unprecedented opportunities to connect with people from around the globe, face-to-face interactions often provide a depth and richness of connection that can be difficult to replicate online. The spontaneity of in-person conversations, the nuances of body language, and the shared experience of being in the same physical space can all contribute to more profound and inspiring exchanges.

As we cultivate inspirational connections, it's also important to be mindful of our own role in these interactions. Just as we seek inspiration from others, we should also strive to be sources of inspiration ourselves. This involves being generous with our own knowledge and experiences, offering encouragement and support to others, and approaching each interaction with authenticity and openness.

The process of finding inspiration through human connections is not always smooth or predictable. It requires patience, openness, and a willingness to embrace uncertainty. Sometimes, the most profound inspirations come from unexpected sources or arise from challenging interactions that push us out of our comfort zones. By remaining receptive to the diverse array of human experiences and perspectives around us, we open ourselves up to a world of potential inspiration.

As we conclude our exploration of the power of human connections in sparking inspiration, it's clear that our interactions with others play a crucial role in our creative journeys. Whether through deep conversations, collaborative projects, or chance encounters, human connections have the potential to broaden our perspectives, challenge our assumptions, and ignite sparks of creativity that can lead to transformative ideas and innovations.

As we move forward, let us carry this awareness of the inspirational potential in our human connections into our daily lives. By cultivating meaningful relationships, practicing active listening, and remaining open to diverse perspectives, we can tap into a rich wellspring of inspiration that will continue to nourish our creative spirits.

In the next chapter, we will shift our focus to another powerful source of inspiration: the world of sound and music. We will explore how the soundscapes that surround us can spark creativity and how we can attune ourselves to the inspirational melodies of life.

Chapter 6: The Soundscape of Inspiration

As we transition from exploring the power of human connections, we now turn our attention to another rich source of everyday inspiration: the world of sound. The auditory landscape that surrounds us is a constant wellspring of creative potential, often overlooked in our visually dominated world. From the gentle rustle of leaves in the wind to the complex harmonies of a symphony, sound has the power to evoke emotions, trigger memories, and spark new ideas.

The relationship between sound and inspiration is as old as humanity itself. Our ancestors found inspiration in the rhythms of nature, using them to create the first musical instruments and compose the earliest songs. This primal connection to sound continues to influence us today, even if we're not always consciously aware of it. As the renowned composer John Cage once said, "There is no such thing as an empty space or an empty time. There is always something to see, something to hear. In fact, try as we may to make a silence, we cannot."

The soundscape of our daily lives is rich and varied, offering a constant stream of potential inspiration. The bustling energy of a city street, with its cacophony of car horns, conversations, and footsteps, can be as inspiring as the serene stillness of a forest at dawn. Even the most mundane sounds - the hum of a refrigerator, the ticking of a clock, or the patter of rain on a roof - can become the starting point for creative thought when we learn to truly listen.

Music, of course, is perhaps the most obvious source of auditory inspiration. Its ability to evoke emotions, tell stories, and transport us to different mental states makes it a powerful tool for sparking creativity. As Friedrich Nietzsche poetically observed, "Without music, life would be a mistake." Whether it's a soaring orchestral piece, a gritty blues riff, or an intricate electronic composition, music has the power to unlock new perspectives and ideas.

But inspiration doesn't only come from pleasant or harmonious sounds. Dissonance, noise, and even silence can be equally inspiring when approached with an open mind. The avant-garde composer Karlheinz Stockhausen pushed the boundaries of what could be considered music, incorporating everyday sounds and electronic noise into his compositions. He believed that "All sounds are equal," challenging us to find beauty and inspiration in unexpected places.

Developing a practice of active listening is key to tapping into the inspirational potential of sound. This involves more than just hearing; it requires a conscious effort to focus on and analyze the sounds around us. Start by taking a few moments each day to close your eyes and really listen to your environment. What sounds can you identify? How do they make you feel? What associations or memories do they trigger?

One technique for enhancing your sound awareness is to create a sound map of your neighborhood or workplace. Spend some time walking around, noting the different sounds you encounter and their locations. This exercise can help you discover sound patterns and rhythms you may have previously overlooked, providing new sources of inspiration.

Another powerful technique is to experiment with sound creation. This doesn't necessarily mean becoming a musician (although learning an instrument can certainly be a rewarding way to explore sound). It can be as simple as using everyday objects to create interesting sounds or rhythms. Try tapping different surfaces in your home, rustling various materials, or even using your voice in unconventional ways. The goal is to become more attuned to the sonic possibilities that surround you.

Silence, too, can be a powerful source of inspiration when used intentionally. In our noisy modern world, moments of true silence are rare and valuable. Many creative individuals, from writers to artists to entrepreneurs, have found that regular periods of silence can enhance their ability to generate new ideas. As the spiritual teacher Eckhart Tolle noted, "Silence is a great teacher, and to learn its lessons you must pay attention to it."

Consider incorporating silent meditation or simply quiet reflection time into your daily routine. This doesn't have to be a formal practice; even a few minutes of sitting quietly and focusing on your breath can help clear your mind and create space for new thoughts and ideas to emerge.

The connection between sound and problem-solving is another fascinating area to explore. Many people find that certain types of music or ambient sounds can help them focus and think more creatively when tackling challenges. This phenomenon, often called the "Mozart Effect," suggests that listening to complex, structured music can temporarily enhance spatial-temporal reasoning.

While the specific effects of music on cognition are still being studied, there's no doubt that many people find certain sounds conducive to creative work. Experiment with different types of music or ambient sounds while you're working on creative projects. You might find that instrumental jazz helps you write, nature sounds enhance your painting, or electronic music boosts your coding productivity.

The world of sound design offers further insights into how we can use auditory experiences to enhance creativity and problem-solving. Sound designers for films, video games, and virtual reality experiences carefully craft audio landscapes to evoke specific emotions and create immersive environments. By studying their techniques, we can learn to be more intentional about the sounds we surround ourselves with and how they affect our mood and thought processes.

One interesting technique from sound design is the use of "sonic branding" - creating distinctive sound identities for products or companies. Think of the famous Intel jingle or the Netflix "ta-dum" sound. These brief audio cues are designed to instantly evoke certain associations and emotions. Try creating your own personal "sonic brand" - a short melody or sound that represents your creative identity. Use this as a trigger to enter a creative mindset when you're starting work on a project.

The intersection of technology and sound offers exciting new possibilities for inspiration. Apps and devices that generate binaural beats or isochronic tones claim to be able to influence brainwave patterns, potentially enhancing focus, creativity, or relaxation. While the scientific evidence for these claims is still developing, many people find such tools helpful in creating conducive mental states for creative work.

Virtual and augmented reality technologies are also opening up new frontiers in sound-based inspiration. Imagine being able to step into a virtual sound environment of your own design, or to layer inspiring sounds over your real-world environment. As these technologies continue to evolve, they will likely offer powerful new tools for exploring the inspirational potential of sound.

It's important to remember that our relationship with sound is deeply personal and cultural. What one person finds inspiring might be distracting or even unpleasant to another. The key is to develop your own awareness of how different sounds affect you and to curate your auditory environment accordingly.

Consider creating a "sound inspiration journal" where you note interesting sounds you encounter throughout your day and any ideas or emotions they trigger. Over time, this can help you identify patterns in what types of sounds most consistently inspire you.

As we conclude our exploration of the soundscape of inspiration, it's clear that the world of sound offers a vast and often untapped resource for creativity and innovation. By developing our capacity for active listening, experimenting with sound creation, and thoughtfully curating our auditory environments, we can open up new channels of inspiration in our everyday lives.

As we move forward, we'll turn our attention to another rich source of everyday inspiration: the world of literature and storytelling. Just as sound can evoke powerful emotions and spark new ideas, the written word has its own unique ability to transport us, challenge our perspectives, and ignite our imaginations. Let's explore how the landscapes of language can further expand our capacity for finding inspiration in the commonplace.

Chapter 7: Literary Landscapes

As we transition from the auditory world of inspiration explored in the previous chapter, we now turn our attention to the rich tapestry of written words. The literary landscape offers a vast and varied terrain for those seeking inspiration, providing not only a wellspring of ideas but also a mirror through which we can examine our own thoughts and experiences.

Books have long been regarded as windows to other worlds, portals through which we can escape the confines of our everyday existence and explore realms limited only by the boundaries of human imagination. Yet, they serve an even greater purpose as catalysts for our own creativity and inspiration. The power of literature lies not just in its ability to transport us, but in its capacity to transform us, sparking new ideas and perspectives that can profoundly impact our lives and work.

Consider the words of the renowned author Neil Gaiman, who once said, "A book is a dream that you hold in your hand." This poetic description encapsulates the essence of literature's inspirational potential. Each book we open is an opportunity to dream, to imagine, and to be inspired. The pages we turn are not mere repositories of information or entertainment; they are launching pads for our own creative journeys.

The act of reading itself is a deeply personal and introspective experience. As we engage with a text, we bring our own experiences, beliefs, and emotions to bear on the words before us. This interaction between reader and text creates a unique alchemy, often resulting in flashes of insight or inspiration that extend far beyond the confines of the story or argument presented. It is in these moments of connection and revelation that we often find the seeds of our own creative endeavors.

Poetry, with its distilled language and evocative imagery, offers a particularly potent source of inspiration. The poet Mary Oliver, known for her keen observations of the natural world, demonstrated how even the simplest of subjects could be transformed into profound reflections on life and existence. Her ability to find wonder in the ordinary challenges us to look at our own surroundings with fresh eyes, to seek out the extraordinary in the everyday.

However, the inspirational power of literature is not limited to fiction and poetry. Non-fiction works, from biographies to scientific treatises, can be equally rich sources of creative sparks. Reading about the lives of historical figures or groundbreaking discoveries can ignite our own ambitions and push us to explore new territories in our personal and professional lives. The key lies in approaching these texts not just as sources of information, but as invitations to engage our own imaginations and critical thinking skills.

One of the most effective techniques for drawing inspiration from literature is the practice of creative reading. This involves more than simply absorbing the words on the page; it requires an active engagement with the text, questioning, analyzing, and connecting ideas to our own experiences and knowledge. By reading creatively, we transform the act of reading from a passive consumption of information into an active dialogue with the author and ourselves.

To read creatively, one might start by keeping a reading journal. This practice allows us to record not just summaries of what we've read, but our own reactions, questions, and ideas sparked by the text. It's a space where we can explore tangential thoughts, draw connections between different works or concepts, and begin to develop our own unique interpretations and ideas.

Another powerful technique is to engage in what might be called "conversation with the text." This involves pausing regularly while reading to ask questions, challenge assumptions, or imagine alternative scenarios. By doing so, we activate our own creative faculties and often stumble upon unexpected insights or ideas. As the writer and philosopher Mortimer J. Adler put it, "In the case of good books, the point is not to see how many of them you can get through, but rather how many can get through to you."

Writing, too, can be a powerful tool for inspiration, even for those who don't consider themselves authors. The act of putting pen to paper (or fingers to keyboard) can unlock thoughts and ideas that might otherwise remain dormant. Free writing exercises, where one writes continuously for a set period without concern for grammar, spelling, or even coherence, can be particularly effective in bypassing our internal censors and accessing our deeper wells of creativity.

For those seeking to broaden their perspectives and spark new ideas, reading outside one's usual genres or areas of interest can be particularly fruitful. A scientist might find unexpected inspiration in a work of magical realism, while an artist might discover new ways of seeing the world in a book on theoretical physics. This cross-pollination of ideas across disciplines often leads to the most innovative and groundbreaking insights.

The power of storytelling, in particular, should not be underestimated as a source of inspiration. Stories have been used throughout human history to convey knowledge, explore complex ideas, and inspire action. By studying the structure and techniques of effective storytelling, we can learn to frame our own ideas in ways that resonate more deeply with others and ourselves.

Literature also serves as a bridge between cultures and across time, allowing us to gain insights from perspectives vastly different from our own. Through books, we can step into the shoes of individuals from different backgrounds, eras, and worldviews. This expansion of our empathetic capacities not only enriches our understanding of the world but can also inspire us to approach our own challenges and creative endeavors from new angles.

The inspirational potential of literature extends beyond the content of the works themselves to the lives and processes of the authors who created them. Learning about the struggles, methods, and breakthroughs of writers we admire can provide both encouragement and practical strategies for our own creative pursuits. Many authors have written extensively about their craft, offering invaluable insights into the creative process and the dedication required to bring ideas to fruition.

It's worth noting that inspiration from literature need not always come from profound or weighty tomes. Sometimes, it's the lighthearted or seemingly trivial that can spark the most unexpected ideas. A clever turn of phrase in a children's book, the rhythm of a nursery rhyme, or the absurd premise of a comedy novel can all serve as springboards for original thought and creation.

As we immerse ourselves in the world of words, it's important to remember that the goal is not just to collect inspirational quotes or ideas, but to use literature as a catalyst for our own growth and creativity. The true measure of a book's inspirational impact lies not in how it makes us feel in the moment, but in how it changes the way we think and act long after we've turned the final page.

In our increasingly digital world, the ways in which we engage with literature are evolving. E-books, audiobooks, and online literary communities offer new avenues for discovering and engaging with written works. While these formats may change the nature of our interaction with texts, the fundamental power of words to inspire remains constant. In fact, these new technologies often facilitate a more interactive and social reading experience, allowing us to share our inspirations and engage in discussions with readers around the globe.

As we conclude our exploration of literary landscapes, we stand poised at the threshold of the digital realm. The next chapter will delve into the vast and ever-changing world of online inspiration, where the written word merges with multimedia experiences to create new forms of creative stimulus. But regardless of the medium, the essence of inspiration through language remains a constant, inviting us to continue our journey of discovery through the power of words.

Chapter 8: Digital Realms of Inspiration

As we transition from exploring the rich tapestry of literary landscapes, we now turn our attention to the vast and ever-expanding digital realm, where inspiration can be found at the click of a button or the swipe of a screen. In this age of unprecedented connectivity, the internet and digital platforms have become powerful tools for discovering, curating, and sharing inspirational content. However, navigating this digital ocean of information requires skill, discernment, and a balanced approach to ensure that we harness its potential without becoming overwhelmed or disconnected from the physical world around us.

The digital age has ushered in a new era of accessibility to inspiration. Social media platforms, blogs, online galleries, and video-sharing sites have democratized the sharing of ideas, art, and experiences. This democratization has led to an explosion of creativity and innovation, as individuals from all walks of life can now showcase their talents and insights to a global audience. The renowned artist Banksy once said, "The thing I hate the most about advertising is that it attracts all the bright, creative and ambitious young people, leaving us mainly with the slow and self-obsessed to become our artists." However, the digital realm has challenged this notion, providing a platform for artists and thinkers who might otherwise have remained in obscurity.

One of the most popular platforms for visual inspiration is Instagram. With its focus on imagery, Instagram has become a virtual gallery where photographers, designers, and artists share their work. The platform's algorithmic feed and explore page can lead users down rabbit holes of inspiration, exposing them to styles, techniques, and ideas they might never have encountered otherwise. However, the curated nature of Instagram can also create a false sense of reality, where only the most polished and perfected images rise to the top. It's crucial for users to approach the platform with a critical eye, understanding that behind every perfect shot lies hours of work, dozens of discarded attempts, and often, sophisticated editing techniques.

Pinterest, another visual-centric platform, has carved out a niche as a digital vision board. Users can create boards on various topics, pinning images that inspire them for future reference. This platform is particularly useful for those seeking inspiration in specific areas such as interior design, fashion, or DIY projects. The ability to save and categorize inspirational content allows users to build a personalized library of ideas that they can revisit whenever they need a creative spark. However, the ease of pinning can sometimes lead to what psychologists call "false progress," where the act of saving ideas gives a sense of accomplishment without actual implementation.

For those seeking inspiration in the realm of ideas and innovation, platforms like TED Talks and YouTube offer a wealth of content. TED's motto, "Ideas worth spreading," encapsulates its mission to share thought-provoking presentations from experts across various fields. These talks can spark new ways of thinking about old problems or introduce viewers to concepts they had never considered before. Similarly, YouTube's vast array of content, from educational videos to vlogs documenting everyday life in different parts of the world, can provide unexpected sources of inspiration. The key is to approach these platforms with an open mind and a willingness to explore beyond one's usual interests.

While visual and video content dominate much of the digital inspiration landscape, text-based platforms still play a crucial role. Twitter, with its character limit, has become a hub for concise wisdom, witty observations, and breaking news that can spark creative thoughts. Medium and other blogging platforms allow for more in-depth exploration of ideas, often providing a space for emerging voices to share their perspectives alongside established thought leaders. The comments sections of these platforms can also be fertile ground for inspiration, as readers engage in dialogue and debate, sometimes leading to new insights and collaborations.

However, the abundance of digital inspiration comes with its own set of challenges. The sheer volume of content available can lead to information overload, making it difficult to process and internalize truly meaningful inspirations. The constant stream of new posts, videos, and articles can create a sense of FOMO (fear of missing out), leading to anxiety and a superficial engagement with content rather than deep reflection. Moreover, the addictive nature of many digital platforms can lead to excessive screen time, potentially disconnecting users from real-world experiences that are often the richest sources of inspiration.

To combat these challenges, it's essential to develop strategies for mindful digital consumption. One effective approach is to set specific times for browsing inspirational content, treating it as a deliberate activity rather than a default way to fill idle moments. This intentional engagement allows for deeper processing and reflection on the content encountered. Additionally, using tools like browser extensions or app settings to limit time spent on certain platforms can help maintain a healthy balance between digital and real-world experiences.

Curating a personalized digital inspiration board is another powerful technique for managing the flow of inspirational content. This can take many forms, from creating private Pinterest boards to using note-taking apps like Evernote or OneNote to save and organize inspiring content from across the web. The key is to develop a system that allows for easy retrieval of saved inspiration when needed, while also encouraging regular review and pruning of collected material to keep it relevant and manageable.

An often-overlooked aspect of digital inspiration is the importance of creating as well as consuming. Platforms like Behance for designers, GitHub for programmers, or personal blogs for writers provide spaces not just to find inspiration but to contribute to the collective pool of ideas. By sharing their own work and insights, individuals can engage in a dialogue with others in their field, potentially sparking new collaborations or receiving feedback that leads to further innovation. This act of creation and sharing can also help combat the passive consumption habit that digital platforms sometimes encourage.

It's crucial to remember that digital inspiration should complement, not replace, real-world experiences. The Danish philosopher Søren Kierkegaard once said, "Life can only be understood backwards; but it must be lived forwards." This wisdom applies to the pursuit of inspiration as well. While digital platforms can provide a wealth of ideas and stimuli, it's the application of these inspirations in real life that leads to true growth and innovation. Therefore, it's important to regularly step away from screens and engage with the physical world, allowing digital inspirations to inform and enhance, rather than dominate, one's creative process.

As we conclude our exploration of digital realms of inspiration, it's clear that the online world offers unprecedented opportunities for discovery and creative stimulation. However, the true art lies in balancing this digital input with real-world experiences and personal reflection. By cultivating a mindful approach to digital inspiration, we can harness its power while avoiding its pitfalls, creating a rich tapestry of influences that fuels our creativity and innovation. As we move forward, let us consider how we can overcome the inevitable creative blocks that arise, even in the face of abundant inspiration. The next chapter will delve into strategies for breaking through these mental obstacles and maintaining our creative momentum in the face of challenges.

Chapter 9: Overcoming Creative Blocks

As we transition from our exploration of digital inspiration sources, we now turn our attention to a challenge that every creative individual faces at some point: the dreaded creative block. In this chapter, we'll delve into the nature of these obstacles, explore strategies to overcome them, and discuss ways to build resilience in the face of creative adversity.

Identifying common barriers to inspiration is the first step in overcoming creative blocks. One of the most prevalent barriers is fear – fear of failure, fear of judgment, or fear of not living up to one's own expectations. This fear can be paralyzing, causing individuals to second-guess their ideas or, worse, prevent them from starting projects altogether. As author Elizabeth Gilbert notes in her book "Big Magic: Creative Living Beyond Fear," "Fear is boring, and other people's fears are even more boring than your own." Gilbert's words remind us that fear is a universal experience among creatives, and acknowledging this can help us move past it.

Another common barrier is perfectionism. The desire to create something flawless can often lead to procrastination or abandonment of projects. This perfectionism is often rooted in comparison – comparing our work to others or to an idealized version of what we think our work should be. It's important to remember that perfection is an illusion, and the pursuit of it can be detrimental to the creative process. As Salvador Dalí once said, "Have no fear of perfection - you'll never reach it."

Lack of time or energy is another frequently cited barrier to inspiration. In our fast-paced world, it can be challenging to carve out dedicated time for creative pursuits. Many individuals feel drained after a long day of work or family responsibilities, leaving little mental or physical energy for creative endeavors. This barrier is often compounded by the misconception that inspiration only strikes when we have large blocks of uninterrupted time – a luxury that few of us can afford in our busy lives.

Environmental factors can also pose significant barriers to inspiration. A chaotic or uninspiring workspace, constant interruptions, or lack of proper tools can all hinder the creative process. Additionally, some individuals find that certain environments – such as a noisy coffee shop or a sterile office – are not conducive to their creative flow.

Negative self-talk and limiting beliefs represent another set of barriers that can be particularly insidious. These internal voices often tell us that we're not talented enough, that our ideas aren't original, or that we don't have anything worthwhile to contribute. These beliefs can be deeply ingrained and may stem from past experiences or societal pressures.

Information overload is a modern barrier that many creatives face. With the vast amount of content available at our fingertips, it's easy to become overwhelmed and paralyzed by the sheer volume of information and ideas. This can lead to a state of analysis paralysis, where we're constantly consuming but never creating.

Now that we've identified some common barriers, let's explore strategies for breaking through these mental obstacles. One powerful technique is mindfulness meditation. By practicing mindfulness, we can learn to observe our thoughts without judgment, allowing us to recognize and release limiting beliefs or fears that may be holding us back. Regular meditation practice can also help cultivate a sense of calm and focus, which can be invaluable when facing creative challenges.

Another effective strategy is to embrace constraints. While it may seem counterintuitive, limitations can often spark creativity. By setting boundaries – whether it's a time limit, a specific theme, or a restricted set of tools – we force our minds to think more creatively within those constraints. This approach can help overcome the paralysis that sometimes comes with having too many options.

Freewriting, or stream of consciousness writing, is another powerful tool for breaking through creative blocks. This technique involves writing continuously for a set period without stopping to edit or censor oneself. The goal is to bypass the critical mind and tap into the subconscious, often leading to unexpected ideas and insights. As Natalie Goldberg, author of "Writing Down the Bones," advises, "Keep your hand moving. Don't cross out. Don't worry about spelling, punctuation, grammar. Lose control. Don't think. Don't get logical. Go for the jugular."

Changing your environment can also be an effective way to overcome creative blocks. This could involve working in a different location, reorganizing your workspace, or simply taking a walk in nature. A change of scenery can provide new stimuli and perspectives, often leading to fresh ideas and renewed inspiration.

Collaboration is another powerful strategy for overcoming creative blocks. Engaging with others can provide new perspectives, spark ideas through dialogue, and offer support and encouragement. This could involve joining a creative group, finding a mentor, or simply bouncing ideas off a friend or colleague.

One often overlooked strategy is the practice of play. As adults, we often forget the importance of play in fostering creativity. Engaging in activities purely for enjoyment, without any specific goal or outcome in mind, can help unlock our creative potential. This could involve anything from doodling and coloring to playing with building blocks or engaging in improvisational games.

Developing a consistent creative routine can also help overcome blocks. By setting aside regular time for creative work, we train our minds to enter a creative state more easily. This routine doesn't have to be rigid – it could be as simple as spending 15 minutes each morning writing in a journal or sketching before bed.

Now, let's discuss developing resilience and maintaining motivation in the face of creative challenges. Resilience is crucial for any creative individual, as setbacks and failures are an inevitable part of the creative process. One way to build resilience is to reframe failure as a learning opportunity. Each setback provides valuable information that can inform future efforts.

Celebrating small wins is another important aspect of building resilience. By acknowledging and appreciating incremental progress, we can maintain motivation and build confidence over time. This could involve keeping a "success journal" where you record daily achievements, no matter how small.

Developing a growth mindset is also crucial for resilience. This involves believing that our abilities and intelligence can be developed through effort, learning, and persistence. With a growth mindset, challenges are seen as opportunities for growth rather than insurmountable obstacles.

Self-compassion is another key component of resilience. It's important to treat ourselves with the same kindness and understanding that we would offer a friend facing similar challenges. As Dr. Kristin Neff, a leading researcher on self-compassion, states, "Instead of mercilessly judging and criticizing yourself for various inadequacies or shortcomings, self-compassion means you are kind and understanding when confronted with personal failings."

Building a support network is also vital for maintaining motivation and resilience. This could involve joining a community of like-minded creatives, finding an accountability partner, or sharing your work with trusted friends or family members. Having people who understand and support your creative journey can provide encouragement during difficult times and celebration during successes.

Setting realistic goals and breaking larger projects into smaller, manageable tasks can help maintain motivation. This approach allows for a sense of progress and accomplishment, even when working on long-term or complex projects. It's important to strike a balance between challenging oneself and setting achievable goals.

Finally, it's crucial to remember that inspiration and creativity often work in cycles. There will be periods of high productivity and flow, as well as times of struggle and apparent stagnation. Recognizing and accepting these cycles can help maintain long-term motivation and prevent discouragement during the inevitable lulls.

In conclusion, creative blocks are a natural part of the creative process, but they need not be insurmountable obstacles. By identifying common barriers, implementing strategies to overcome them, and developing resilience, we can navigate these challenges and emerge stronger and more inspired. As we move forward to the final chapter of our exploration, we'll look at how to integrate these insights and practices into our daily lives, creating a sustainable approach to living an inspired life.

Chapter 10: Cultivating an Inspired Life

As we conclude our exploration of finding inspiration in the commonplace, it's fitting to discuss how we can integrate these insights into our daily lives. Chapter 10 focuses on cultivating an inspired life, building upon the techniques and perspectives we've explored throughout this book.

Creating a life filled with inspiration is not about waiting for those rare, earth-shattering moments of enlightenment. Rather, it's about developing a mindset and set of practices that allow us to find sparks of inspiration in the everyday world around us. This chapter will guide you through the process of integrating inspiration-seeking practices into your daily routines, creating personal rituals for sustained creativity, and sharing the inspiration you find with others.

Integrating inspiration-seeking practices into daily routines is perhaps the most crucial step in cultivating an inspired life. It's about making the search for inspiration a habit, as natural as brushing your teeth or checking your emails. Start by setting aside dedicated time each day for inspiration-seeking activities. This could be as simple as spending ten minutes each morning observing the world around you with fresh eyes, or taking a different route to work to expose yourself to new sights and experiences.

One effective practice is to keep an inspiration journal. Each day, write down at least one thing that sparked your interest or curiosity. It could be a conversation overheard on the bus, an interesting cloud formation, or a new idea that popped into your head while doing the dishes. The act of recording these moments not only helps you remember them but also trains your mind to be more aware of potential sources of inspiration throughout the day.

Another powerful technique is to incorporate mindfulness into your daily routine. Mindfulness, at its core, is about being fully present in the moment, which is essential for noticing the subtle inspirations that surround us. Try practicing mindful eating, really savoring the flavors and textures of your food. Or engage in mindful walking, paying attention to the sensation of your feet touching the ground, the rhythm of your breath, and the sights and sounds around you. As you become more mindful, you'll find that inspiration can strike at the most unexpected moments.

Creating personal rituals for sustained creativity is another key aspect of cultivating an inspired life. Rituals provide structure and consistency, creating a fertile ground for inspiration to flourish. These rituals can be as unique as you are, tailored to your personal preferences and lifestyle. For some, a morning ritual of journaling or sketching while sipping a cup of coffee sets the tone for a day of creative thinking. For others, an evening ritual of reading poetry or listening to inspiring music helps to process the day's experiences and spark new ideas.

Consider creating a dedicated inspiration space in your home. This could be a corner of your living room, a small desk, or even just a shelf. Fill this space with objects that inspire you – books, artwork, natural objects, or mementos from meaningful experiences. Make it a ritual to spend time in this space regularly, allowing yourself to be surrounded by things that spark your creativity.

Another powerful ritual is the practice of regular idea generation. Set aside time each week to brainstorm ideas, regardless of their practicality or relevance to your current projects. The goal is to exercise your creative muscles and keep your mind open to new possibilities. You might set a target of coming up with 10 new ideas each day, or spend 15 minutes each morning free-writing whatever comes to mind. As author and creativity expert James Altucher suggests, "The idea muscle atrophies within days if you don't use it. Just like any other muscle in your body." By making idea generation a regular ritual, you ensure that your "idea muscle" stays in shape, ready to provide inspiration when you need it most.

Incorporating movement into your daily routine can also be a powerful ritual for sustained creativity. Many great thinkers throughout history have sworn by the creative benefits of walking. Friedrich Nietzsche once said, "All truly great thoughts are conceived while walking." Whether it's a morning jog, an afternoon stroll, or an evening yoga session, find a form of movement that works for you and make it a regular part of your day. The combination of physical activity and change of scenery can often lead to unexpected bursts of inspiration.

While personal practices and rituals are crucial, cultivating an inspired life also involves sharing and spreading inspiration to others. As Maya Angelou beautifully put it, "Nothing can dim the light which shines from within." When you share your inspirations, you not only reinforce them for yourself but also create a ripple effect, potentially inspiring others in turn.

One way to share inspiration is through regular conversations with friends, family, or colleagues about ideas that excite you. Make it a habit to ask others what's inspiring them lately, and be generous in sharing your own sources of inspiration. These conversations can lead to unexpected collaborations and new perspectives that further fuel your creative fire.

Consider starting a blog or social media account dedicated to sharing your daily inspirations. This not only creates accountability for your inspiration-seeking practices but also allows you to connect with like-minded individuals who can further enrich your creative journey. Remember, what seems ordinary to you might be profoundly inspiring to someone else.

Volunteering or mentoring in your field of expertise is another powerful way to spread inspiration. By sharing your knowledge and passion with others, you not only inspire them but often find yourself reinspired by their fresh perspectives and enthusiasm. As Albert Einstein once said, "If you can't explain it simply, you don't understand it well enough." The process of explaining your ideas to others can lead to deeper understanding and new insights for yourself.

Organizing or participating in creative meetups or workshops is yet another way to cultivate and spread inspiration. These gatherings provide opportunities to learn new skills, exchange ideas, and connect with other creative individuals. Whether it's a book club, a painting class, or a tech meetup, regular engagement with a community of like-minded individuals can provide ongoing motivation and inspiration.

As we cultivate an inspired life, it's important to remember that inspiration is not a constant state. There will be days when inspiration seems elusive, and that's perfectly normal. The key is to trust in the practices and rituals you've established, knowing that they will guide you back to a place of inspiration. As author Elizabeth Gilbert writes in her book "Big Magic," "The work wants to be made, and it wants to be made through you."

Cultivating an inspired life is about creating an environment – both internal and external – that nurtures creativity and curiosity. It's about developing the habits and mindsets that allow you to see the extraordinary in the ordinary, to find those everyday sparks that can ignite great ideas. By integrating inspiration-seeking practices into your daily routines, creating personal rituals for sustained creativity, and sharing your inspirations with others, you open yourself up to a life rich with creative potential.

Remember, inspiration is not just about those rare "eureka" moments. It's about cultivating a sustained state of openness and curiosity that allows you to find meaning and beauty in the world around you. As you move forward from this book, carry with you the tools and perspectives we've explored. Let them guide you in your ongoing journey of discovery, as you continue to find inspiration in the commonplace and transform those everyday sparks into the fuel for a richly creative and fulfilling life.

Conclusion

As we conclude our journey through "Everyday Sparks," it's clear that inspiration isn't confined to grand moments or rare occurrences. It's all around us, waiting to be discovered in the most ordinary aspects of our lives. From the gentle rustle of leaves to the hum of a busy city street, every experience holds the potential to ignite our creativity and spark new ideas.

Throughout this book, we've explored various sources of inspiration, from nature and art to human connections and digital realms. We've learned techniques to sharpen our senses, cultivate mindfulness, and overcome creative blocks. These tools empower us to see the world with fresh eyes and find meaning in the seemingly mundane.

The power of everyday inspiration lies in its accessibility. We don't need to wait for a lightning bolt of genius or a life-changing event to fuel our creativity. By developing an observant mindset and embracing curiosity, we can transform our daily routines into wellsprings of innovation and personal growth. The stories and case studies shared in this book demonstrate that groundbreaking ideas often stem from the most unexpected places.

Ultimately, living an inspired life is a choice we make each day. It requires practice, patience, and a willingness to see beauty and potential in the world around us. By integrating the techniques and perspectives discussed in this book, we can create a life rich with creativity, purpose, and continuous growth. Remember, inspiration is not just about what we see, but how we choose to see it.

As you close this book, carry with you the knowledge that every moment holds the potential for inspiration. Your next great idea might be hiding in plain sight, waiting for you to notice it. Stay curious, stay open, and let the everyday sparks of inspiration guide you towards a more creative and fulfilling lifeb.

BARKON LEGESSE

Write your day

Write your day

BARKON LEGESSE

Write your day

64

<u>Write your day</u>

65

BARKON LEGESSE

<u>Write your day</u>

Write your day

67

BARKON LEGESSE

Write your day

<u>Write your day</u>

BARKON LEGESSE

<u>Write your day</u>

Write your day

BARKON LEGESSE

Write your day

<u>Write your day</u>

73

BARKON LEGESSE

Write your day

74

<u>Write your day</u>

75